Speak Softly & Carry Your Own Gym Key

D0910954

A Female High School Principal's Guide to Survival

Anna T. Hicks

CORWIN PRESS, INC.
A Sage Publications Company
Thousand Oaks, California

Copyright ©1996 by Corwin Press, Inc.

All rights reserved. No part of this book may be reproduced or utilized in any form or by any means, electronic or mechanical, including photocopying, recording, or by any information storage and retrieval system, without permission in writing from the publisher.

For information address:

Corwin Press, Inc.
A Sage Publications Company
2455 Teller Road
Thousand Oaks, California 91320
e-mail: order@corwin.sagepub.com

SAGE Publications Ltd.
6 Bonhill Street
London EC2A 4PU
United Kingdom

SAGE Publications India Pvt. Ltd.
M-32 Market
Greater Kailash I
New Delhi 110 048 India

Printed in the United States of America

Library of Congress Cataloging-in-Publication Data

Hicks, Anna T.
    Speak softly & carry your own gym key : a female high school
principal's guide to survival / Anna T. Hicks.
        p.   cm.
    Includes bibliographical references (p. 71)
    ISBN 0-8039-6383-1 (cloth). — ISBN 0-8039-6384-X (pbk.)
    1. Women school principals—United States. 2. High school
principals—United States. 3. Sex discrimination in education—
United States. 4. School management and organization—United
States. 5. Hicks, Anna T. I. Title.
LB2831.92.H53   1996
371.2'012'082—dc20   95-40561

This book is printed on acid-free paper.

    97 98 99 00 10 9 8 7 6 5 4 3 2

Corwin Press Production Editor: S. Marlene Head

Contents

Foreword

Dear Anna,

In his 1909 classic, *The American High School*, John Franklin Brown had the following to say about the importance of gender among the qualifications for the high school principalship:

> Generally speaking, men make better principals than women, especially in large schools. They are stronger physically; they possess more executive ability; they are more likely to command the confidence of male citizens; they are more judicial in mind; they are more sure to seize upon the essential merits of a question; they are less likely to look at things from a personal point of view; they are likely to be better supported by subordinates; and simply because they are men, they are more likely to command fully the respect and confidence of boys. (pp. 241-242)

His book was reprinted seven times during the 6 years following its original 1909 publication date, so one would assume that Mr. Brown's opinions about the leadership of American high schools made perfect sense to a significant proportion of the book-buying public in the first decades after the turn of the century. In truth, this fact shouldn't be all that disturbing, given the tenor of the times. The country was still mired in the backwaters of the Victorian period; ladies continued to wear dresses down to their ankles, while their big strong men were off fighting those evil Germans on the battlefields of Europe.

But Anna, what you reveal to all of us in a very personal and compelling way in *Speak Softly & Carry Your Own Gym Key* is most disturbing. After reading your account of your 4-year career as the principal of a large suburban high school, one is forced to conclude that as a society, we really haven't progressed very far during the past century in regard to our attitudes about women in leadership roles. Apparently, a substantial majority of men, and sadly, even women, still believe that in addition to "knowing when to leave," ladies should be content to be the "fairer" sex, to nurture and support, to look pretty, smell nice, speak softly, and most important, follow rather than lead. After all, what could a woman principal possibly want with a set of keys to the gymnasium?

I suppose that the blatantly sexist attitudes that are revealed in your book shouldn't come as a surprise to me. I've seen it all around me as my career in educational leadership has unfolded. As you know, I chaired a national study of American high schools and their leaders for the National Association of Secondary School Principals (NASSP) at the end of the 1980s. The results of that study reaffirmed what had already been learned about women school leaders in all the previous studies of its kind—when it comes to leadership of America's secondary schools, women are underrepresented, underpaid, and underappreciated.

Anna, it is one thing to be forced by your book to recognize the prevalence of ugly sexist attitudes at the very heart of the one American institution that is charged by society with the responsibility for promoting equality of opportunity for all to pursue the American dream. It is quite another to admit to myself that I am and have long been a part of the problem.

Albeit unwittingly, almost all males must share some responsibility for not permitting or not actively promoting women to take their rightful places among the leadership of

America's schools. On behalf of males everywhere, I want to tell you that we haven't failed in this regard because we are evil; it is because we are ignorant. I have more than 50 years of experience as a male, but not one single minute as a female. I have been a member of the brotherhood all my life; my friends, my teachers, my mentors have all been men just like me. Unfortunately, this fact has blinded me and millions of other males and made us insensitive to the barriers that women leaders must somehow negotiate in order to lead. Anna, please believe me when I tell you that we just didn't know any better.

I am grateful for my professional experiences and close associations with women leaders during the past 10 or 15 years, because they have allowed me to see things a little more clearly. But Anna, I am still learning, and I badly needed to read your book. Although I know you wrote this book for women who aspire to the secondary principalship, I truly believe that men need it just as much as, if not more than, women.

In the first place, many of the truths that you reveal in this book with your beautiful use of metaphors are universal in nature. All of us who are striving to be effective, reflective school leaders can grow enormously from sharing your introspections about what it really means to be a leader. After reading your book, I know that I will think a good deal more about the importance of "tending the students' garden" rather than the superintendent's.

A second reason men need to read your book is that they already have the keys to the gymnasium. Until men are ready to share "all the keys" with their female colleagues, American schools will be denied the full measure of executive leadership that women can bring to the table. And you know as well as I do, Anna, that never have American secondary schools needed a major infusion of leadership the way they do at this moment. Women are unquestionably the most abundant and best source of leadership available to fill this need. I truly believe that your book can help us realize and utilize that great storehouse of largely untapped potential.

John Franklin Brown has been dead a long time now; it's time we buried some of his outdated ideas with him. Thanks for a very moving and enlightening experience!

Sincerely,
LEONARD O. PELLICER
Chair, Educational Leadership and Policies
University of South Carolina

About the Author

Anna T. Hicks is an educational consultant, writer, and clinical faculty member in the Department of Educational Leadership and Policy at the University of South Carolina, where she teaches classes in school personnel administration and leadership. Her experience includes teaching English and journalism at the high school level and serving first as an assistant principal and language arts coordinator and then as her district's first female high school principal. She holds a B.A. in English from Columbia College (1974) and an M.A. (1978) and a Ph.D. in Educational Administration from the University of South Carolina (1992). During her 21-year career in public education, she was a runner-up for South Carolina Teacher of the Year and was twice named Best Principal in a readership poll sponsored by the *State* newspaper. She has written and spoken in the areas of women in administration, instructional leadership, and school reform and change.

*To my mentors for their gentle wisdom
and other collectibles.
To Larry for his wisdom, insight, and love.*

Prologue

Early in my first year as my school district's first female high school principal, I experienced what was to become the metaphor for my ambivalent journey in the profession—the quest for my own gym key.

Employed in the district at the time was a true Southern good ole boy who played the role of maintenance coordinator. He learned quickly to smile patronizingly and say to all who asked his assistance, "There is no money," or "We're understaffed." I was always "Miss Anna" when he called, even on the morning when he phoned about changing the locks on the gym to protect the new wooden floor.

"You have a security problem down there. Everybody in town has a key to the gym. We're changing the locks and issuing keys that can't be duplicated. I'll send enough for the custodians, coaches, and an assistant principal," he said.

"What about my key?" I asked innocently.

"You don't need a key," was his response. "Just open the vault and get that one if you need it."

"Help me understand," I said, retaining the control all Southern ladies are taught in order to avoid showing anger, "If I get a call in the middle of the night and need to get in the gym, I must first unlock the vault and get the key?"

"That's right," he said, "we've made enough keys," as he hung up the phone.

I immediately called his supervisor, an associate superintendent, who promised me a key and apologized for his employee's lack of human relations skills. I reminded him that the other two male high school principals would probably not have had such difficulty.

Within 30 minutes, my key had been delivered, but with instructions from the maintenance supervisor that I had to sign a statement saying I would be responsible for damage to the gym floor. The maintenance supervisor has since resigned amid questions involving missing inventory, and I have yet to sign such a statement.

My ambivalent journey in this profession has revealed to me the uniqueness of the high school principalship with its traditions, assumptions, and rites of passage that often erect barriers for women. The journey, which ended after 4 years in the position, often was incredibly lonely, but I was fortunate along the way to experience the mentoring of special people, particularly a few enlightened men who celebrated my femininity in a traditionally male leadership role. They allowed me to speak softly and carry my own gym key.

1

A Single Woman With Three Children: A Principal?

I never planned to be a principal. In the small Southern town where I grew up, my options were teaching and nursing (my mother's vocation). The older of two children, I stepped on the achievement treadmill early in life, adding As and other honors to walls and scrapbooks.

I probably became a teacher because I enjoyed school and excelled in it. And I loved English. If I could be an English teacher, I thought, kids would love me as I loved many of my teachers. Also, my mother always had reminded me that teaching was a good career for a woman who had to work and who wanted summers and afternoons with her children. And the world was definitely going to hell because women were working too much.

I began my career as a student teacher in the school where I eventually served as principal. Yes, I paid my dues—department head, assistant principal, district coordinator of language arts. Within 16 years, I had married, had three children, divorced, and earned my Ph.D. in educational administration by the age of 40.

I've had very little difficulty making most decisions. Relying strongly on intuition, when the principalship of the school where I had spent most of my career was advertised, I knew I would apply but told no one because I thought perhaps I should talk myself out of it. The reason? I didn't think I could handle losing it and I didn't think a female would be hired. But the advice of a friend and something inside possessed me to prepare the vita and letter of application.

The interview process was 3 long months of surprises and disappointments. I soon began to realize that a few men had a problem envisioning a female in the job, but many women did also. One female friend stopped me in the grocery store to describe last night's bridge game, where my ability to take a gun away from a student had been debated.

One day in the superintendent's office, I realized that he perhaps had the most concerns. He reminded me that if I were selected, I would not make much more money than I was making currently. (I knew better because I had reviewed the salary schedule.) He then asked me why a single woman with three children would want to be a high school principal. His words stung. I realized he was trying to get me to withdraw.

When we left for spring break, I realized I had just experienced blatant discrimination. I had two choices: withdraw, because it appeared I had no chance, or stay and make him turn me down. I chose the latter and sat down to compose a letter to the superintendent detailing my reasons for wanting the job and respectfully requesting that my single-parent status be a nonissue. Writing was always my solace and the letter energized me. He never acknowledged its receipt.

As the interview process drew to a close, two male parents wrote letters on my behalf, citing the need for more females in leadership positions as role models for their daughters. The female school board member, however, began involving herself by demanding a national search. No one in the state was good enough and she definitely didn't want me.

In the third and final interview before a committee of parents, teachers, and district administrators, the superintendent removed his glasses, stared at me intently and asked, "Just how tough are you?" I used my response to address my single-parent status as evidence of my personal success rather than a negative issue in the selection process.

The search committee chose me, but only after a male candidate from Virginia turned the job down. I never would have known I was second choice if the female board member hadn't called the press and complained about the lack of a thorough search and the loss of the first candidate. Those headlines hurt and still do. A male teacher whom I confronted about his ineptness when I served as associate principal for instruction wrote an anonymous letter to the newspaper complaining that the only reason I was chosen was that the teachers on the interview committee were friends of mine. The superintendent, however, from the day the board approved my appointment was a strong supporter and always set me up to be successful. I have missed him more than he will ever know since his retirement.

On July 1, 1991, I moved into the principal's office. With no money to redecorate or re-cover the black leather chairs, I hung my favorite Van Gogh, set my porcelain doll on the desk, and placed my children's pictures where I could see them. From home, I brought a Delft ginger jar for the top of the credenza and hung a mirror—something this male office had never seen. Despite the feminine touches, however, it would take some time for the staff to adjust to a woman in the office.

2

Free Advice and Other Throwaways

Educators are fortunate that many people who often have no idea what they're talking about are most willing and eager to advise the principal. I was privileged to receive endless advice.

Early in the job, the associate superintendent for personnel, a veteran in the district who had always played the well-meaning fatherly role with me and remains a good friend, called me in for his traditional "How to Look Like a Principal" speech. He stressed the importance of the power-suit look, the proper length of skirts, and the importance of a professional hairdo. I asked if there was anything wrong with my hair. He was quick to say no, but I wondered.

Always eager to please, I went shopping for suits at a local well-known "dress for success" boutique and tried on one suit after another until I realized I simply wasn't a suit person. And I wasn't a suit person because I wasn't a conformist. I never had been, especially when it came to dress. I viewed dressing as a creative expression of myself, and a suit said nothing about me.

I then visited my hairdresser and said, "Make me look like a principal." He rolled his eyes and gave me an asymmetrical cut. So much for looking the part.

Another important aspect of looking the part of a high school principal is learning to use and carry a walkie-talkie with the savvy of a local deputy. It was especially important in my school because the local sheriff's department monitored our channel. The first walkie-talkie I held was quite heavy, so I traded it for a slim, lightweight version and began practicing. Soon I was hooked. There is incredible power in being able to communicate and summon in such a fashion. The head custodian finally became used to being summoned by a female and learned to answer. I also discovered quickly, however, that if there were times when I didn't want to be found (and yes, there were a few), I could simply turn it off. People would assume I was busy and could not be disturbed.

In attempting to look and act like a high school principal, I realized there were certain things I would be unable to do. Though becoming a part of the largely male administrative team was important to me, I lacked certain common traits of these men:

1. I was 10 years younger than most.
2. I had never been a coach. The closest I had come was being a newspaper sponsor.
3. I drove neither a truck nor any four-wheel-drive vehicle.
4. I had no desire to put notches in my belt for every child expelled.
5. I had never been to Fat Buddy's, the local wings-and-beer hangout.
6. I believed that teachers and students were meant not to be controlled, but rather empowered.
7. I wanted to focus on the vision and future of the school rather than "It's working; don't fix it."

In short, after analyzing the Myers-Briggs Personality Types of each member of the administrative team, I soon realized I was an INFP (Introverted Intuitive Feeling Perceptive), a Joan of Arc, a quester, a catalyst, leading a group of ESTJs (Extroverted Sensing Thinking Judging) and ISTJs (Introverted Sensing Thinking Judging), and that one lone proponent of Theory Y would have an uphill battle against Theory X. Somehow, the scale didn't seem evenly balanced. I wondered—I don't look the part and may not even act the part as expected. Am I in the right profession?

3

Gentle Wisdom and Other Collectibles

The alienation and loneliness of the female high school principal are at times overwhelming. Having experienced a very lonely childhood, I have never mastered being able to ask for help, but instead have played the role of helping others. I credit my survival in the high school principalship to individuals who knew me well enough to recognize my need. They were powerfully aware that even on a good day a principal makes decisions that might not please everyone and might leave the principal feeling lonely and vulnerable.

Though there were members of my staff that I valued and cared for deeply, there were many times when only someone outside the building would do. My female mentor, ironically, at first doubted my abilities to succeed in administration. When the previous principal wanted to hire me as his associate principal for instruction, this woman questioned my ability to stand up for the instructional program. However, over the years she came to know and respect my abilities, and to this day she is someone I can call on who has been there, first in her experience as a middle and elementary school principal, and then as associate superintendent for instruction, now retired.

When she served as interim superintendent, we suffered together when I placed on administrative leave a highly respected teacher who subsequently resigned as a result of charges related to the sexual harassment of female students. We "took the heat" together as female administrators perceived as "out to get" a man whose intentions were supposedly misperceived. With the support of our district's female attorney—a woman of great courage, intellect, and confidence—and the board, we exercised our professional and ethical responsibilities not to discuss the case with the staff or the press for fear of embarrassing the teacher's family. His resignation vindicated our actions.

Another mentor was my doctoral committee and dissertation chairperson, a gentleman scholar experienced as a superintendent and professor. As a student in the master's program, I took his General Organization and Administration and Finance courses only because I needed electives. He was an incredible teacher who lured me into the challenge of school administration. As my dissertation chair, he was a caring but demanding "guide on the side" who kept me going with such wisdom as "A dissertation is like a marriage. Once you commit, you must see it through."

My friend and favorite cheerleader was another professor on my doctoral committee. He recruited me for the Ph.D. program and acted as my unofficial adviser through those years. He made me laugh and he celebrated my uniqueness as a female administrator. In the middle of my graduate study, I traveled to Washington, DC with his policy class to study educational policy at the federal level. One cold, icy day in Washington, I emerged from the National Gallery of Art, where I had purchased a Van Gogh print. I encountered on the mall a homeless man attempting to build a fire and cover himself with cardboard. Behind him limousines cruised by and the powerful political elite walked on, continuing the business of government, oblivious to the poverty at their feet.

My mentor processed this experience with me over dinner and enticed me to develop a policy analysis paper on the education of homeless children. It was my favorite professional work, a possible dissertation topic with ethnographic research possibilities that I was unable to reconcile logistically.

But the experience and his wisdom pulled from within me a firm commitment to be a champion of the underdog and to believe in the dignity and worth of all humanity. He went on to coach me through my dissertation and published an article with me in *Executive Educator*.

My third mentor was a chaired research professor whose dissertation preparation class produced chapters 1 and 3 of my dissertation. When I think of him, the word that comes to mind is *awe*—awe of his incredible mind, his ability to make meaningful connections among seemingly unrelated circumstances and events, and his vision for the future. I feared him at first but then came to feel confident and comfortable in his presence. He solidified my tendency never to be comfortable with the status quo.

With luck, in every female high school principal's life, there is a supportive significant other. After a failed marriage, I wasn't hopeful, but he appeared anyway in the form of a soul mate—someone so much like me that he challenged me to examine myself and the doubt that encumbered me. He celebrated my leadership role and was neither threatened nor intimidated by my success. As a physician and therapist, he, too, worked in a highly visible role where patients, like students and parents, demanded individual time and attention. And, like me, he felt great frustration with the system and with the realization that the only way to survive was detachment. I love him deeply.

Why were most of my mentors male? I could speculate about several reasons, but the reality is that each in his own way was like my father, who died of cancer in 1985. In everyone's life there should be at least one source of unconditional love. My dad was mine. A man with a giving nature and no pretense, he never scolded me for wrongdoing. His silence was always enough. Much more powerful were his positive support and pride. I wonder what he thinks of me now.

Each of my mentors somehow stroked my self-esteem and gave me the wisdom and courage to detach to view the big picture.

4

Small Minds
Can't See the
Big Picture

We are not the systems in which we participate."
Those are the words of Drs. Thomas and Patrick
Malone in *The Art of Intimacy* (1987, p. 271).

My experience in the principalship has taught me that a
key to survival is detachment from the various systems in
the school community and the realization that some people
will never see the big picture. The principal's role is one of
stepping back to reconcile competing interests.

A powerful system from which the principal must detach is the faculty. In the era of site-based management, such
detachment sounds contradictory, but in reality it is necessary for the principal to give up control in order to empower
teachers. My high school faculty was, for the most part,
intelligent, experienced, and independent. Secondary school
reform would not occur without their buy-in and support.
For this reason, I gave the following decisions to the faculty:
the assignment of all teacher duties, the design of a modified
schedule, the implementation of interdisciplinary curriculum, and the use of Channel One.

We eased into the reform movement. As a suburban
middle-class high school with the highest test scores in the
state, we battled the prevailing power of the status quo, and
my role with the faculty was as one who raised the questions

and provided resources. If I had "taken charge and man-dated," I would have immersed myself in a control system where I would have drowned. I was the facilitator on the side who repeatedly asked, "In whose best interest are we making this decision?" The answer was, I hoped, "The students'."

Ironically, another system from which the principal must detach is the students. To do otherwise is to risk the tendency to parent those for whom there are no advocates. I've served in this role and failed. Twin girls in our school came to my attention for excessive absences and possible denial of credit for Carnegie units. Ten minutes with the pair confirmed my suspicions: a dysfunctional family, a mother with a black belt in codependency, an alcoholic father, and a bleak future for the girls. I plunged in with referral to our at-risk program, second chances for excessive absences, an arrangement for free medical care, and my giving my beeper number to one twin who feared for her safety in her home.

I lost them both—one to substance abuse, the other to pregnancy, both searches for unconditional love. I was per-haps too close. As a mother of twins, I felt a bond. As a principal, I knew they were victims and worth saving. They dropped out before graduation. The at-risk coordinator, their other advocate, and I consoled each other and commis-erated. As I awarded diplomas at commencement, I noticed their absence in the Ss. But one principal and one school are powerless against an entrenched family system. I still won-der about them.

Yes, parents are indeed powerful, and the parent systems within the school can be its greatest strength and its greatest weakness. In my school, I enjoyed tremendous parental sup-port for fundraising and extracurricular activities. Unfortu-nately, in the high school setting, such support was often fragmented and narrowly focused. I had many booster clubs—athletic, band, ROTC, chorus, academic quiz team. Together, they raised more than $150,000 a year for the school, but too often their visions were specifically focused on their children and one single activity.

The Band Booster Club was a unique experience. When I became principal, the band director was an incredibly tal-ented, charismatic man who was revered by students. He resigned in the middle of the year for personal reasons, leaving the Booster Club parents in the middle of a war against each other over the direction of the music program. The Booster Club had been paying the director extra money for work "beyond" his contract, and the district found itself in a dispute with the Booster Club and the state Ethics Commission over the compensation. I found myself in the midst of a controversy involving the hiring of a new band director, who came in only to confront parents who demanded a superior marching band at the expense of a balanced instrumental music program. The year of transition with the new director was long and turbulent. At one point, discouraged with warring factions in the Booster Club, I took two couples who had been at each other's throats to breakfast in an attempt at conflict resolution. After tears, name-calling, blaming, and anguish, I realized I had failed. There are indeed parents whose entire lives revolve around their children's extracurricular participation in high school, and I as principal was powerless to assist them in developing their own separate lives. There are also some individuals on this earth who are never happy unless they are creating chaos or are in the middle of it. To this day, these two families speak to me but not to each other. I grieve for this failure.

Still another system from which the principal must detach is the district office. Having worked at the district level as language arts coordinator for 2 years, I developed a full appreciation for this need. District administrators experience the dilemma of an ongoing question: What is my real authority? As coordinator of language arts, I saw myself as a facilitator, a support system for the schools. As principal, I expected the same. As a result, what I perceived as mandates from the district office became challenges to question. When I heard that gifted students who did not complete their summer reading automatically would be dropped to a lower-level class, my response was, "Not at our school. We'll simply lower their grade." When word was sent down as to where our file servers would be located for implementation of the district technology plan, I allowed my media specialist to express her need for a different location for the file server. My greatest frustration with the district office was not so much with individuals, but with a system that never really defined site-based management. Decisions were left to the schools unless they became controversial. The most controversial decisions were reserved for the board. Sometimes it was hard to predict which decisions would be controversial. However, one sure bet was that if "terminally gifted" parents objected, board approval was essential. Some high schools in the state eased into block scheduling with the trust and confidence of the community. My school's attempt met with media attention, personal attacks on the principal, and despair and discouragement for teachers who wanted to move the school forward.

And finally, the need to detach from the administrative staff itself became most powerful early in the job. With a staff largely dominated by individuals who believed that teachers and students were people to be controlled and not trusted, I soon realized that balance was essential. I firmly believed that there were indeed talented, trustworthy members of the faculty and student body who could take a vision and run with it. All I had to do was place these individuals in key leadership roles and allow them to move ahead. The result was a faculty endorsement for Channel One with school board approval, followed by a pilot year of implementation and successful evaluation. Teachers can, and indeed do, prove their professional expertise to lead change efforts.

The female high school principal faces unique challenges in her attempts to detach from various systems: The faculty, the students, and parents groups are formidable and often entrenched systems. However, high school principals must continue their commitment to seeing beyond these often narrow interests to take care of all children. My greatest challenge in detaching was the world of high school athletics.

5

The Brotherhood:
The World of Athletics

The toughest system for the female high school principal is the male-dominated world of high school athletics. This kingdom unto itself is a powerful entity, especially in the South, where football generates the revenue for other sports and where most principals and athletic directors are former coaches.

When I became principal, it was clear that the head football coach and athletic director was uncomfortable with a female in the main office. Added to his discomfort was the fact that because he had been hired 14 years ago by a previous superintendent and not by a principal, he found it difficult to stop bypassing the principal and going straight to the district office when he wanted something. One of my first official trips to the district office was to visit the superintendent and his associates to respectfully remind them that their first question to the athletic director should be "Have you talked with Anna first?"

Despite his sexist nature and skill at manipulation, the athletic director was in reality a good man who on many occasions did what he could to teach me the rules and regulations of the state Athletic League. I realized early in the job that I could do what a few other female principals had done and simply delegate the responsibility to the athletic director with instructions to "keep me informed."

However, after attending my first meeting at the state level and being the only woman there, I was disturbed at things I overheard: the bashing and joking about another female high school principal in the state whom several considered "pushy," open disdain for the sport of soccer, and talk of decisions that I felt were not in the best interests of children. Yes, I stayed and continued to attend these meetings. Luckily, within a couple of years I became friends with two male principals in the state who were not threatened by my presence, who knew my athletic director might not give me complete information, and whose schools were similar to mine and faced similar problems.

The power in the State League is committees. As a female, I was appointed to chair the Volleyball Committee, one with no power and no rule controversies. Our biggest discussion in 3 years was changing the date that record sheets were due for playoffs. The power committees were football and basketball. There were no female members until one was added to the basketball committee. The rosters reflected the movers and shakers in high school athletics—the many outspoken former coaches, as well as the behind-the-scenes politicians. Decisions were usually made before meetings via a sophisticated telephone network.

My third year as principal, I graduated to the Program Committee because my athletic director was president of his state association, and our spring meeting was a joint venture. I chose this opportunity to raise a question I had raised before. Why was cheerleading not considered a sport under the high school league? The answer? "The superintendents don't support it."

"But our principal's survey last year showed majority support. Let's go back to the superintendents," I suggested.

One principal volunteered to call the superintendent in charge of this issue. He has yet to make the call 2 years later. Then our committee voted to bring in a speaker from another state where cheerleading functioned as a sport. I was excited that there might be some recognition for this largely female activity.

Never miss a meeting. I missed the next planning meeting of the Program Committee, and a member called to tell me that my agenda item had been removed. He speculated that the League office, not eager to take on the regulation of another sport, had been influential in removing it.

At our spring meeting, to my great delight and surprise, a male principal raised the issue again from the floor, calling for a show of hands that revealed overwhelming support for cheerleading as an official sport. The League director heard the message. The following fall, I was appointed to a state committee to develop a proposal for cheerleading as a sport. The South Carolina High School League Executive Committee approved, and cheerleading was declared an official sport in the state, to begin in 1996.

With football often dominating the budget focus because it generates the most revenue and supports other sports, it often falls to the principal to take care of other sports. My 4 years as principal were full of "picking up after" and sometimes overruling decisions made concerning the use of space. To a football coach, the stadium and practice fields are covered with sacred turf not to be contaminated by soccer shoes or band students' Nikes. However, to parents of these students, who pay taxes in the district, space should be shared. Much of my time was spent negotiating the sharing of space to be certain everyone had a place to play and practice.

At the end of my third year as principal, the athletic director decided to take advantage of the district's retirement incentive option. However, his plan, which he announced to me, was to give up coaching and continue working as athletic director for the maximum salary allowed under retirement regulations. When I questioned this plan, he informed me that the decision would not be mine but would be made at the district level.

The only way I could deal with his audacity and my anger was to write an emphatic letter to the interim superintendent, informing her of his intentions and my adamant opposition to such a plan. I knew the Booster Club was ready for a change, and I stated in the letter that such a proposal was not in the best interests of the school. Someone evidently convinced the athletic director of the same.

I then began what turned into a 4-month search for a new athletic director and head football coach. No other personnel experience comes close to my adventures in this search. From early in the process, the men in my school and district assumed I would want and need lots of assistance, because I supposedly knew "nothing" about football. However, I met informally with athletes, coaches, and Booster Club parents to gather input for the search. The job description that resulted actually was simple: We wanted a good coach, a good athletic director, and a good man. Finding him wasn't so easy.

Two of the best coaches and athletic directors in the state applied for the job. Our new superintendent and board were not willing to pay what it would have taken to hire them. In addition, these two coaches, confident of their status and reputations, insisted on jobs for their wives, reduced work-loads for their staffs, and permission to fire current coaches who wouldn't conform. I felt as though I was negotiating with corporate executives. They withdrew their names.

It also became clear that other coaches wanted to apply but were waiting to be asked. The motive was twofold: They wondered, "Am I good enough to be asked?" and they wanted to be able to tell the folks back home that they were recruited and possibly use the situation to get a raise.

Throughout the process, despite my attempts to main-tain confidentiality, a persistent leak to the press resulted in articles and headlines speculating on our difficulty in filling the position. Frustrated with the local sportswriter, when he informed me that he would have to speculate if I wouldn't break confidentiality, I responded with, "Speculation is all you've done anyway."

Greatly discouraged, I called the League office in a neighboring state and asked for the name of a good coach and athletic director. It was a fortunate phone call. After the first interview, I knew I had found him. This man was quiet, humble, completely devoid of pretense, and a former phys-ics teacher. It was clear that he loved kids and football and that he was prepared for the challenge. Nothing was final, however, until the superintendent interviewed and ap-proved him. My last superintendent also chose to interview and approve the hiring of any person applying for any administrative position I filled—a unique version of site-based management, I suppose.

I'll never forget the parent who called to tell me the new coach had visited her home. He has probably made more home visits than a hospice nurse. He was worth the hassle.

6

The Pom-Pom Wars

I have a Ph.D. in educational administration. Nothing in my doctoral program prepared me to deal with cheerleaders. I was forced to draw on my own experience as a cheerleader, as the parent of a cheerleader, and then as the principal of cheerleaders.

Another high school principal once told me that his greatest controversy his first year concerned the cheerleaders' shoes. I remember wondering how that could be. Another colleague fired his cheerleader sponsor and parents marched in on the school board in protest. I went virtually unscathed by cheerleader controversy until my third year as principal. The experience must be a rite of passage for the profession.

Having been a cheerleader for a while myself, I understood the mystique. It makes one visible and accepted in school. It provides a group of friends who have common goals. It says to one's peers, "I'm cool." But cheerleading has changed since my high school experience. Then we simply had to look pretty and be voted on by our peers. Being a klutz was okay. Popularity was more important.

Cheerleading in the 1990s requires it all—looks as well as athletic and dance ability. The competition is keen and only the best-trained survive tryouts. Our tryouts were held after a week of training and practice. Finals occurred before a panel of university cheerleaders who did not know the applicants. Tryout week was a tense time. Parent tempers were smoldering. At one time, I contemplated hiring a deputy but my athletic director assured me he could handle the cheerleader mothers. Thankfully, my home phone number was not listed in the directory.

Located in our community was a highly successful dance studio with a nationally recognized dance team. The girls represented the best in jazz, gymnastics, and performance training. If one of these girls chose to try out for cheerleader, her success was virtually guaranteed. In my third year as principal, I stumbled on a controversy that had been brewing for years. The fear of these highly trained dancers by other students dying to be cheerleaders brought out the worst in many. One cheerleader hopeful called the dance studio to determine summer competition and practice times, hoping to negotiate different times for the cheerleading squad. The intent, of course, was to ensure that dance-team girls would be shut out. Fate stepped in, however, and this young lady did not make cheerleader.

Also during tryouts, one senior cheerleader, a former dance-team star, gave an impassioned speech on commitment. Directed toward the dance-team girls, the message was, "You can't do both, and don't bother to try." For reasons I never will be able to fully investigate or prove, camp week was scheduled during the dance team's national competition. The dancers came to me, concerned, wondering whether or not to try out because camp was required. I encouraged them to go ahead and try out while I investigated alternatives.

The questions in my mind were: (1) Was camp deliberately scheduled to exclude these girls? and (2) Could we legally require camp in the summer as a prerequisite to being a cheerleader? I contacted our attorney and asked her to review our entire cheerleader constitution. That I would even investigate the matter angered non-dance-team cheerleader hopefuls and their parents. I responded to phone calls for 2 days, and one Friday night was completely ruined by a parent who obtained my home phone number.

The attorney's response was, yes, camp can be required. Cheerleading is a privilege and not a right. She suggested a reasonable attempt for that year to find alternative dates. I tried, but alternative dates were not available. In addition, we had already placed a $300 deposit for camp. I informed the sponsor that everyone must go or be off the squad.

War began. The parents of two dance team members as well as the studio director appealed to the superintendent. We all met. The situation was clearly one with no winners. Our attorney advised a compromise. Though our constitution said that camp was required, it did not explicitly state that failure to attend would result in dismissal from the squad. The compromise was this: The girls would attend camp for 2 days, leave for their competition, and return to camp. We would clean up the constitution for next year.

I called the cheerleaders and sponsors together to inform them of the decision. I stressed that although I wanted to hear their concerns, I was there to put out a fire and that when the meeting was over, the ashes would not even be smoldering. Instead, I expected a new spirit and sense of teamwork to emerge from the ashes. There were questions, tears, and anger. Two of the young ladies were undoubtedly the most disrespectful adolescents I encountered in my career. When I met their mothers later, I realized who their role models were. I took the opportunity to speak to the all-female group and say the following:

> What I have observed in this experience is something that reminds me of a sad reality. All too often, women do not take care of each other. Rather than supporting each other, they engage in petty competitive jealousy as they climb the ladder to success. That ladder is hard enough for women to climb. I challenge you as representatives of your female generation to fix what my generation hasn't.

The Pom-Pom Wars were over, or so I thought. Peace might have followed if parents had not become involved. One cheerleader ran home to Daddy one day, claiming that the others had verbally harassed and threatened to drop her as they met off campus without a sponsor present. I investigated the charge but could not obtain enough evidence to take action. This cheerleader also broke a long-hidden school cheerleader tradition—the "Confidence Code," which the girls used to share secrets and eventually to lie to their parents, sponsors, and the administration. The penalty for a girl who violated the code was to require her to grab her crotch in front of everyone at a pep rally. I had heard enough. I moved the cheerleaders completely under the control of the athletic department, threw out the constitution, and directed the athletic director to treat them like any other athletic team.

Debriefing the experience with my eldest daughter, who at the time was a cheerleader in another district high school, I asked her to promise me that if I ever became an obnoxious cheerleader parent with no life of my own, she would call me on it and sign me up for therapy.

7

Taking Care of
the Customers

If we could just get rid of these kids, we could get some work done," is what I often wanted to say to teachers and administrators who complained about students.

I am amazed that in the field of education, where all of our energy, planning, and funding should be directed to students, students are still often the underdogs, and those of us who champion their cause must continue to remind the adults of the purpose of our work. After 20 years of working with adolescents, I am convinced that many of the adults who work with them neither understand nor appreciate their true nature or potential.

At a public hearing held at my school on the subject of our district's human sexuality curriculum, a parent complained that our school's award-winning student newspaper was full of articles that reflected a "How-dare-you-tell-me-what-to-do"attitude. I simply shook my head and said silently, "Don't you understand that is exactly the attitude the student editors and writers are supposed to have?"

The adolescent who questions and challenges is asking the significant adults in his or her life two questions: "Do I have permission to disagree with you?" and "If I disagree, will I still be loved and accepted?" These two questions form the basis of my dealing with students.

The student newspaper is an example. I never censored or exercised prior restraint over the publication. Instead, a publications board composed of teachers and students was formed for occasions when questions arose. The students often disagreed with the administration in their editorials. Giving them this permission, however, resulted in their responsible reporting and their showing both sides of an issue. If parents called to complain about the paper, I referred them to the staff and encouraged them to write a letter to the editor. I even wrote letters to the editor as a way to communicate with the student body. When the students were upset about a proposed move to block scheduling, I wrote a letter explaining what happens to a school going through the change process in an era of reform.

In addition to the student newspaper, I have developed opinions related to student dress and the battles we lose with kids. During my first year as principal, the assistant principals appealed to me to do something about the board policy forbidding kids to wear hats in the building. Their concern was that they were spending all their time taking off hats when their energy could be better directed toward class cuts, tardies, and more serious offenses. I heard their concern. Recognizing that the cultural taboo, especially in the South, against wearing a hat in the building was just that—cultural—I approached the other principals who agreed and then the school board with a request to change the policy, pointing out that no research existed that showed a relationship between hats and poor discipline. It was a major, humiliating defeat. Senior citizens called board members in outrage. One female board member stated passionately, "We all know that children who wear hats are not well-disciplined." The board voted 7-0 to retain the policy. I was left in lonely defeat, as supporters of the effort had allowed me to lead the fight alone. It was then that I became the designated troublemaker.

So the assistant principals and I continued to play games with the kids. They wore their hats to school and we made them angry by taking the hats off. And the culture was preserved, with the fervent hope that all discipline problems would disappear (one day in Camelot).

Student dress will continue to be a challenge for high school principals as our culture becomes more diverse. The Southern middle-class high school where I served as principal was not immune to increasing diversity. We were originally a White-flight suburban school, but our African American population doubled within 5 years, and with this growth came my need to function more than ever as an active advocate for minority students.

The first racial issue to confront me as a principal centered on the crowning of the school's first African American Homecoming Queen. Away in Philadelphia at a Coalition of Essential Schools forum at the time, I returned to stories of jeers and taunts as well as objects being thrown at the new queen by students and, worse, by parents. Then an anonymous note appeared, expressing concern that the new queen allegedly was attending our school illegally and actually lived in another district. By board policy, I was bound to investigate the matter, so I called her in. Though I knew the charge was maliciously motivated, I could not gather enough evidence to verify her residency. The only other option would have been to get in my car and physically check up on the situation. I chose not to do so. I determined that a higher cause was the healing of racial tension that was escalating over the events of Homecoming and was polarizing African American and White football players.

I took the problem to the students. I first wrote a letter to the editor in the student newspaper, expressing my disappointment with the students' response at the Homecoming game. Suggesting that such actions did not represent the feelings of the majority of the student population, I challenged them to love and care for each other.

I then organized a multicultural student group that came together to form what they called the Uniteam, symbolized by their T-shirt design of a hand of color and a white hand converging, with both forefingers in a "Number 1" design of unity. I discovered the magic of putting kids in a room, feeding them pizza, and giving them the racial problem to solve. Their solution was a cultural awareness assembly featuring an African American speaker—a teacher, Harvard graduate, and a native of the state. His presentation was honest, dynamic, and controversial.

At the end of the day of the assembly, an angry White parent appeared in the main office demanding to see the principal about the "liberal assembly." His rage was such that the veins in his neck pulsed with anger. One of my male assistant principals, fearing for my safety, accompanied me as I invited the parent into my office. He refused to be seated at my invitation to sit down and talk. I chose to be seated anyway as he glared at me. The assistant principal, sensing the parent's potential for violence, remained standing as the man proceeded to blast me, the liberal school, the liberal assembly that promoted liberal attitudes, and our liberal student newspaper. He demanded to know why a White speaker did not present "the other side." All my responses went unheard in the midst of his rage and threats to go to the school board and the press.

His child graduated and, to this day, I wonder at the humiliation she must have felt as she waited for her father in the main office. A year later, when the battle over the presence of the Confederate flag on the top of the South Carolina statehouse was raging, I was driving in a semirural area about 10 miles from the school. Suddenly, to my right I saw a sign—KKK Meeting—and next to the sign were two Klansmen in white robes and hoods. I had lived in the South all my life and had heard the stories of Klan meetings, but this was my first encounter. I wondered if the parent I tangled with was in attendance that day.

In addition to racial issues arising from increasing diversity, religious issues were in question. After taking the heat for outlawing prayer at graduation, the school board revised its policy and decided to allow prayer at graduation if it was student initiated, student written, and student delivered in a nonsectarian, nonproselytizing manner. As an Episcopalian principal in the Bible Belt, I often found myself in sympathy with those students and their parents who did not hold to conservative religious views. As luck would have it, the first year of the new board policy allowing prayer at graduation, the senior class president was Hindu. He came to me because a student had approached him about having prayer at graduation and, as class president, he had the burden of initiating the vote of the senior class. If the vote was favorable, the formation of a student committee to write the prayer would be his responsibility. A talented, caring young man, he was overwhelmed with the charge. "Dr. Hicks," he said, "I thought all I had to do for graduation was welcome the audience and design the senior T-shirt." My response was, "It's hard for me, too. We'll go through it together."

He rose to the occasion. The senior class sponsor worried and agonized. I reminded her that the kids would take care of it. All would be well. A Jewish student came forward, threatening to challenge the legality of the board policy allowing prayer. He called the local chapter of the American Civil Liberties Union but could not generate much interest in the case. In the end, he joined the committee to write the prayer and pronounced their efforts nonsectarian and non-proselytizing. He still made headlines in the state, claiming religious harassment in his homeroom. Our office was flooded with phone calls. One elderly lady called to say that she was praying for me and the school. I told her I needed all the prayer she could muster.

Kids take care of things. The senior class elected an African American student to deliver the prayer. The prayer itself, though never equal to the eloquence of King James English, was a sincere expression of praise and thanks to family, friends, school, and a higher power. Because school board policy required the advice and counsel of the principal, I simply edited the prayer for grammar, changing none of the sentiments. Graduation went well. Lightning didn't strike. And once again, the students solved their own problems.

Educators who discount and dismiss the insight and value of the opinions of adolescents in their school experience lose sight of a precious resource. The innocence and idealism of youth, combined with their healthy skepticism of adult actions and decisions, can guide and direct us if we will only listen. We are not always able to give adolescents what they think they need. We are capable, however, of valuing their worth and their being. May I never live to believe otherwise.

8

Not My Kid!

I remember at one point in my principalship verbalizing that I much preferred working with kids to working with adults. My experience with discipline issues during my last year in the principalship brought the reason into focus. I kept a mental list of parents I wanted to commit to mandatory therapy.

The suburban middle-class community in which I lived and worked was at times in major denial. They demanded strong discipline. The mandate was so strong that when a new superintendent was hired who led the development of a tough new discipline code that allowed for no exceptions to rules, there was no protest from parents, even though the new code was highly publicized and reviewed. After all, if we were tough, schools would be safe places and learning would be our major focus. Yes, parents liked the code—until school started and suddenly a few discovered that the code was not just for other people's kids. It was for all kids!

I then began to see fully how parents are often the most powerful enablers of their children's continued misbehavior. The thinking seems to be, "My child wouldn't do this. If I admit he did, I'll look bad. I can't be a bad parent." The inability of parents to separate their self-esteem from their children's actions led to some classic parental lines I mentally collected during my time as principal:

"My child never lies."

"That teacher is out to get my child."

"She was late because I was running late. I'll serve her detention hall for her."

"He acts that way because a teacher taped his mouth shut in the first grade."

"If he says he had one beer, that's all he had."

"That beer on the floor of the car was mine, not my kid's. I planned to drink it tomorrow on the way back from the airport."

"I have no problem with my child carrying hundreds of dollars around campus."

"My child has a constitutional right to a parking place."

"If my child argued with the teacher, she has my permission. I've always taught her to stand up for herself."

"I admit he was wrong, but my child doesn't need to be suspended. This is too harsh."

"You're a mother, too. Don't you have any heart?"

"I can't believe you're sending my child to in-school suspension. I hope you're able to sleep tonight."

"The governor is a friend of mine, you know."

I watched one mother wage a powerful crusade when her son was caught drinking. In her denial, she insisted he didn't need counseling or intervention. She and her friends tried the "wear-down-the-school-board" strategy by appearing at several meetings in a row, begging, crying, and appealing in public participation. The principals watched in horror as the board on a 4-3 vote almost reversed itself to change the drinking policy. Luckily, cooler heads prevailed and the parent group lost the energy for its battle. Five months later, the student was arrested twice in 1 day for possession at the beach.

Politics can even enter the picture when some little darlings have been naughty. In the South, the public schools have never been immune to the power of the "good ole boy" system. I learned this firsthand when I suspended one young man. His father, though admitting his son's guilt, was most concerned about the possible blight on his heretofore spotless discipline record. He was the nicest angry parent I ever encountered. I never knew who was so well-connected—him or his attorney—but whoever possessed such powerful connections managed within a week's time to run us through all appeal avenues. I found myself standing before the state Supreme Court with the entire appeal policy under fire.

Our policy was upheld, but the parent was most gracious. His energy for the fight amazed me, and I wondered whose battle this really was.

Through difficult discipline situations, a principal must never lose her cool. I've been yelled at, cursed at, threatened, and ignored. On a few special occasions, parents have actually thanked me for holding to standards of discipline. Recently, I saw on an office door something I perhaps needed for those tough cases—a unique version of "The Serenity Prayer":

God, grant me the serenity to accept the things I cannot change, the courage to change the things I can, and the wisdom to bury the bodies of those people who really pissed me off.

9

Turf Issues and Other Explorations of Space

Having a sense of place is a powerful need of employees in a high school.

We often define ourselves and our roles by the size and location of our space, as well as whether or not others can enter our space. As principal, I was no exception.

I followed a principal who frequently and willingly relinquished his office to assistant principals to use for their convenience. Because their offices were located all over the building, the rationale seemed to be that if they found themselves in the main office, dealing with students, the principal's office was much closer than their own. This principal had also maintained a neat, immaculate desk. My desk, however, was usually in disarray even 10 minutes after my patient secretary had cleaned it up. I often left personal information on the desk that no one else needed to see.

I vividly recall the experience of returning from a meeting to find my office occupied by an assistant principal handling a discipline matter. For some reason, I felt personally invaded. The feeling was so powerful that I politely opened the door, indicated that I needed my office, and requested that the occupants continue their discussion elsewhere. On another occasion, I was in my office with the door closed, in conference with the associate superintendent for personnel. One of my assistant principals, thinking I

32

wasn't there, took his master key and proceeded to unlock my office for his own use until he found, to his embarrassment, that it was occupied. My secretary informed me that while I was on vacation, one of my assistant principals used my office each day and particularly seemed to enjoy sitting behind the principal's desk. Her own office, however, was off-limits to others.

Teachers in my school were especially protective of their space. The school was a facility simply inadequate to meet the space and service needs of the student population and the faculty. As a result, teachers fought for space and for furniture to equip the space. Some battled openly, some attempted to manipulate the system, and some simply stole things.

In a large high school, one never leaves behind anything of value over the summer. It's not that the kids steal it. It's that it might appear in the fall in someone else's room. Teachers even consider district property theirs and guard it fiercely. One teacher, determined not to lose her favorite desk chair, marked it in several inconspicuous places. Sure enough, when she returned in August, it was missing. Hell hath no fury like a teacher whose space has been violated. As she marched down the hall, everyone knew she was on a mission and that nothing would stop her. She suspected who had stolen her chair, found it, retrieved it, and promptly told him to "go to hell."

In all high schools, there exists certain "sacred space." Such space is often associated with the temperament of the occupants. In the school in which I worked, sacred space was most easily identifiable when the occupant failed to leave a key for a substitute staffer. If the head custodian, the department head, and even the principal don't have a key, then the space is defined as "sacred." It also applies when the occupant has decided to change the locks and has "neglected" to inform anyone. In my school, the sacred spaces were the choral room, the ROTC room, and the band room.

At times, teachers feel they don't have enough space, so they go searching for more of it. One of the greatest battles for space in my school occurred when we were suddenly blessed with a new computer lab—and no room for it. The solution was simple; someone would have to float. Before the administration could even begin to find a solution, one department head decided to begin the search. One day, she slyly strolled into a teacher's room in another department, started scouting the area, and announced, "I'm shopping for a lab." The news traveled fast, the lounges were "abuzz," and I ended up mediating among two department heads and one teacher in tears.

The most sacred turf for many high school teachers is the master schedule. Unfortunately, many high school master schedules are still factory models where kids travel every 50 minutes with no meaningful connections along the way. Nothing waiting in the real world for kids in any way resembles such a system. Yet this teacher-friendly way to organize the day is so deeply entrenched that its defense and protection bring out the worst in teachers.

It took me 4 years as a principal to finally move the school to even a modified block schedule. When several teachers became truly excited about the idea and were ready to forge ahead with a semester block schedule, the saboteurs went to work. Three teachers used the captive audiences of the kids in their classroom to distort the plan and encourage the students to have their parents call the district office and the school board to complain. One teacher was the mastermind behind a student petition against the proposed schedule. It appeared for a while that one of the best schools in the state might become the great keeper of educational dinosaurs. However, a fine teacher, who later became District Teacher of the Year, chaired a committee of students, teachers, and parents to develop a modified block schedule that eventually received board approval.

Remembering those teachers who sabotaged the effort and who fought so hard to protect their turf, I am reminded of the wise words of a former personnel director I worked for: "We are not an employment agency. We are here for kids."

10

How Does Your Garden Grow?

I worked under several superintendents in my 21 years in public education. What I discovered about each of them was a survival obsession with "If it doesn't look right, I won't look right."

When I began teaching, a colleague made curtains for her portable classroom. The superintendent, who was adamant that shades on all windows must be drawn at the same level, drove by the portable and extolled the virtues of this teacher for her interior decoration and its appearance from the outside.

Little did he know that her students were working to beautify the portable while studying British literature. These energetic adolescents planted an English garden in front of the portable. They loved and tended the garden. Though she was pleased with the students' interest, the teacher couldn't quite understand their fascination until one day she discovered they had planted marijuana among the flowers.

Another superintendent, the one who hired me as principal, taught me a great deal about "how things look." I came to understand that many superintendents view the principal's job as one of maintenance—to keep things looking right so the superintendent can maintain his or her job. Given the high turnover rate of superintendents, such a survival strategy is understandable.

This superintendent was an expert in landscaping. His own yard was a *Southern Living* showplace. Every spring, an agenda item at the principals' meeting was "Roundup," with a reminder to keep the grass cut and use Roundup on the weeds. The superintendent would ride by my school frequently to keep tabs on any superfluous growth and remind me of the importance of maintaining the image of the "flagship high school of the district."

I found myself irritated at first with his obsession, but found myself slowly becoming just like him. I would ride by the school on my way to church and make mental notes to the head custodian. I even found myself pulling weeds in the school's flower garden.

My experience with superintendents was that they were often so busy looking for the weeds, they seldom saw the flowers. A principal spends a great deal of time in a balancing act between pulling the weeds and wondering how to get the superintendent to look at the flowers.

For another superintendent, the weeds were hats in the building and trays left on the cafeteria tables. He once told me, "I don't care how much you know about instruction, Anna; if you can't keep the hats off the kids' heads and the trays off the tables, you'll never be a successful high school principal." I remember thinking to myself, "Does it matter that our SAT scores are the highest in the state and increasing every year, that our school is deregulated, that our special-education program was named one of the five best in the nation?" Yes, it probably mattered—but not to him if someone had just called to complain about hats and trays.

The best example of the importance of "how things look" is high school graduation. For some reason, graduation is a strong measure of principal success. The community, board, and superintendent often judge the year and the principal by the success of the event.

The three high school principals in our district went into stress overdrive as graduation approached. We commiserated by phone, threatened seniors with work detail if they acted out, wrote letters to their parents about expected behavior, and held our breath as "Pomp and Circumstance" began.

One fellow principal in the district experienced the graduation from hell—the ultimate nightmare: the beach ball incident. In the middle of the ceremony, a beach ball appeared and was tossed from senior to senior, until it bounced to a coach who made the sad mistake of hitting it back to the class. The ball eventually hit a school board member in the head and the coach was later reprimanded. It took the superintendent 2 years to recover. He muttered obscenities every time the subject was mentioned. The principal took heat from parents who complained that their children were not allowed to "enjoy their graduation." Damned if you do, damned if you don't.

I have come to realize that if the superintendent planted a garden outside his office and maintained it in a state of immaculate readiness for inspection by Martha Stewart, no one would care. Therefore, he had to have a more public display of his passion for things lovely and green. And that meant he must become invested in what the principal heretofore thought was *her* garden, that is, her school.

I could have easily anticipated the annual "Roundup" speech, gotten a 2-week head start on the weeds, and waited patiently for the accolades. But I came to realize that to head off the weeds at the pass would have deprived the superintendent of his role as "honorary superintendent of grounds" and he might have traded this benign activity for a more malignant obsession with something I would have perceived as a threat to push my "not-good-enough woman" button.

The annual "Roundup" was the benign metaphor of one superintendent's need for "things" to look good as an overall reflection of his leadership. Conversely, the hats-and-lunch-trays incidents were the malignant obsessions of another superintendent's personal insecurity and fuel for his tendencies to be verbally abusive. As a principal, I spent a great deal of time tending the superintendent's garden, often looking for affirmation and approval, which were at times elusive.

I often wondered, "What does it take to be good enough?"

11

Making the Grade: What Does It Take to Be Good Enough?

Being the first female high school principal in my district was sometimes lonely and frightening. The need for affirmation was powerful, especially for one whose childhood script was written toward tangible proof of being "good-enough." The message was that an individual accumulated honors and accolades as proof of her worth. The reality was that such tangible rewards were never enough. Being good enough is validated only through acceptance of self. I'm slowly learning this fact.

Prior to entering administration, I was chosen District Teacher of the Year and was runner-up for State Teacher of the Year. Looking back, I realize this recognition was the honor that brought me the greatest joy. The state competition required me to compile a scrapbook on my career, with endorsements from students and colleagues. It was difficult to approach these individuals. I felt as if I were asking for letters telling me how great I was. Now, as I look back, I realize that teachers desperately need that affirmation and should never have to ask. The scrapbook occupied a special shelf in my office during my years as principal and was there for a lift on dark days.

As a principal, I soon learned that affirmation was conditional, subject to whom I pleased when I made any given decision. Sometimes it even came before a decision in the hopes of influencing me. The older I became and the longer I stayed in the principalship, the more I sought to protect myself from such influence. When one believes, as I do, that most people do the best they can most of the time, the disappointments in others can be painful. To have one's own motives questioned is even more painful.

My third year as principal was especially difficult. The personnel action I had to take in the sexual harassment case left me an easy target for male comments about "those female administrators." My battles with the athletic director and the search for a new one left me weary and frustrated. I was fighting yet another battle that was building in me so much resentment that I knew I would have to take some risks to resolve it. But taking those risks might put my friends and colleagues in jeopardy. The battle was over salary.

When I was hired as a new principal, I was placed on the salary schedule at a lower level than the male high school principals because I had no previous principal experience. Even though I ran the largest school and earned my Ph.D. the next year, there was no provision for movement on the schedule, especially when the board for several years had offered no increases for administrators. State law required that I be the highest-paid employee in the school: I made about $1.00 more per day than the athletic director. I never questioned the salary situation, however, until later.

One summer, after opening my July 15 paycheck, I noticed that the gross was less than usual. I called payroll at the district office and talked to a secretary who informed me that my salary had been lowered $800 because one of my assistant principals had retired, and that it would be lowered $3000 more if the athletic director retired. Angered and hurt that no one had told me and that any principal's salary could be lowered, I called each associate superintendent as well as the interim superintendent. No one seemed to know about my situation, but a couple of people acknowledged that because administrators had received no raises for 2 years and there was no movement on the schedule, the possibility existed.

That week at a principal's luncheon, I took on my "designated troublemaker" role and raised the issue with my colleagues. I discovered to my surprise that attempts had been made to lower other principals' salaries when their school sizes declined but that the previous superintendent had the salaries reinstated. I approached the interim superintendent with this information. She wrote a letter on my behalf to the board, but the board took no action. Things were becoming clear. No one seemed to feel passion for this issue but me. I did something I had never done—I approached the board chairman with my concern. He was sympathetic, but felt nothing could be done until a new salary study was conducted. I felt I had nowhere to turn.

As budgets for the next year were prepared and copies of each school's budget were placed in our school, I was too busy to be concerned with any budget but mine. However, one of my associate principals approached me with her concern that my salary was much lower than that of three other principals in the district. I then reviewed the other principals' salaries and was disheartened to see that the other two high school principals would each make $7,000 more the next year and the one middle school principal would make $4,000 more.

Resentment is a killer. Rather than give in to it, I seized the opportunity when a new superintendent was hired. When I approached him with my concern, he said he never heard of the possibility of lowering a principal's salary. He then invited me to write a letter to the board with whatever I wanted to say. His listening and his invitation to write began to soften my hard feelings and bitterness. But I knew the greatest battle was ahead—with the board. One board member had made it very clear that he felt not only that administrators were overpaid but also that there were too many of us. At meetings, the "We the People" antitax group sat in the audience to cheer his actions.

The matter went before the board in executive session. When the board returned to open session, five of the seven members voted not to lower my salary. Two members abstained. Those abstentions hurt at first, but as time went on, I began to realize the meaning. An abstention is a way to (1) avoid taking sides and (2) vote against the issue but not the person.

The district recently completed a salary study in my last days on the job. The consultant recommended a $15,000 increase for me. The local press printed current salaries under the Freedom of Information Act and the inequities came to public attention for the first time. My phone started ringing. Friends were outraged. The superintendent received calls and told me that when people asked why my salary was so much lower than the salaries of the male high school principals, his reply was, "I don't know." My only satisfaction is that the outside consultant recognized and addressed the inequity. My sadness is that my contribution as a 21-year employee wasn't valued.

It is unfortunate but nevertheless a reality of capitalistic culture that one's worth, one's "good-enoughness," is measured in dollars and cents. A very highly paid baseball player once admitted that his salary was ridiculously high. He quickly added that it was not a matter of how much he was paid, but how much he was paid in relation to his colleagues. If others are paid more, it means they are better ballplayers.

In my situation, the personal message was that the other principals were "better ballplayers." For a woman, the message was that women are inherently not as proficient at playing ball as men. I hope we do not have to wait until a woman breaks into the major leagues before school systems insist on gender equity in salaries.

12

The District House Salad: Selected Fruits and Nuts in Season

I met some incredibly crazy people in my years in the principalship. Every principal has her own selected "fruits and nuts." I had quite a collection, but four were very memorable.

My cafeteria manager refused to retire. Even an early-retirement incentive couldn't entice her. I never understood why anyone so miserable would want to perpetuate her own misery. She would go for a period of days as pleasant as any good Southern hostess, but then she would yell at the kids and they would scream back. Her cafeteria temper tantrums became well-known, and the kids named her "that vegetable-line lady."

I finally convinced her that an outdoor vending cart with pizza and other kids' favorites would boost cafeteria sales. Our students loved the warm South Carolina sun and preferred the grounds to the cafeteria. She relented, but then the Great Paper Chase began.

The issue was napkins. The students who brought their own lunches and ate outside asked for napkins. The cafeteria manager went ballistic and demanded that someone be on duty to determine who got a napkin and who didn't. The assistant principals ended lunch duty one day shaking their heads in frustration and asking where they should direct their energy—class cuts, drugs, tardies, or napkins. I contacted the district food service manager, who informed the vegetable-line lady that losing a few napkins would not break the budget.

The craziest teacher I ever supervised was someone the female teachers described as "the last person I'd ever be married to." "Mr. Sleaze," as he became known, had greasy, slicked-back hair and cynical, evil eyes that repelled many people. Students either liked or despised him. He frequently digressed in class to subjects that bordered on the inappropriate and offended different religious and ethnic groups. He was slick, though, and whenever observed, he played it straight. Mr. Sleaze worked also as a homebound instructor in two or three school districts and often sneaked off campus for his other job. One day, however, he got caught. We had a fire between the floors and evacuated the building. I was away at a meeting at the time. When I returned, I determined that it was safe to send the students back to class. Because Mr. Sleaze had left campus, his students were unattended. He was not happy about his reprimand.

Another character was the teacher I described as "the only man Will Rogers never met." He still wore his 1950s crew cut and oxford-cloth shirts. This teacher usually greeted his students at the beginning of the year with promises to give grades that would "thin out the Beta Club" and with reminders that their previous teachers hadn't taught them what they needed to know, so he would have to start over. Kids liked him or they feared him, many to the point of tears. Each summer I was greeted in the grocery store or at church with requests to "be certain my child doesn't have that teacher." His professional goal was to be remembered as tough but good. Unfortunately, he built a legacy of "mean, insensitive, and stubborn." One day in a postobservation conference, realizing he was in denial about what I was trying to tell him, I looked at him directly and said, "You will never teach my children." I realized then that any principal can measure the quality of a teacher with one simple question: Would I place my child in that teacher's class?

The most infamous character I ever encountered was a school board member who came to be known as "The Weasel."

A stickler for the budget and for detail, he loved to play "I gotcha" and catch anyone employed in the district in a mistake. His great obsession was lights. He traveled to various schools, especially on weekends, checking to see which lights were burning, and he would call the district office on Monday morning to report. I often said that I needed to increase the school's personnel budget to add a light manager.

This same board member did not approve of women in leadership roles. He decided he definitely didn't like me. I soon began to realize that he was checking on my whereabouts and my comings-and-goings to and from school. One day he appeared at school and announced to one of my associate principals that I was choosing to arrive at school as late as 9:00 a.m. in the summer and that he had checked at the district office and there were no meetings scheduled. He said the reason he knew was that I was not in my assigned parking space. The interesting thing was that I had no assigned space. By my decision, only our Teacher of the Year had that privilege.

One day, he even reported to the superintendent that I was not at school on time. I told the superintendent to remind him that I arrived each day at 7:00 a.m. for bus duty, that I had no assigned space, and that because I had traded cars, he might not know what he was talking about. I was not his only female target. Another district principal found him hiding one night in the bushes of her school, hoping she wouldn't see he was checking to be certain she had locked the doors to the school. She shined her headlights on him and waved.

This board member also took delight in humiliating and embarrassing employees in open session in board meetings. Teachers became afraid to make presentations for fear he would attack them. The last presentation I made to the board concerned a new modified block schedule proposal for the school. After the teachers presented their portion, they asked that I respond to questions. I'm glad the teachers did not have to endure his antics; I simply argued with him. Being a short-timer gave me tremendous courage.

Thankfully, most fruits and nuts were somewhat seasonal, and they seemed to take turns creating chaos. Unfortunately, there is one "season" in public education where they all bloom at once and entice their supporters out of the woodwork. This season is known as school board elections. People who run for school board generally fall into one of three categories:

1. Honest, dedicated citizens who have a sincere desire to serve their community
2. Persons with no interest in serving on school boards but who need to start their political career in a fairly high-visibility role
3. Special-interest gurus who have a black belt in scapegoatism and a master's degree in finger-pointing

For the latter, voter apathy is their greatest ally, and they can get elected on a single issue—lately, taxes. Prior to that it was "whipping these liberal educators who are trying to brainwash our kids into New Age religion into shape." These "tax savers" may be the biggest bloomers in the whole garden. Many of them are graduates of the Reagan School of Voodoo Economics, whereby one promises more for less and any problem that requires substantial expenditure of money is handled by pretending it does not exist. Hence the buildings in my school stayed in a progressive state of decay while the tax-relief special interest group said the real problem was too many administrators.

I never did figure out how to deal with these people effectively, which is probably a tribute to my own sanity. And so far, at least, I have not felt any compelling desire to gather data by hiding in the bushes.

13

Men, Women, and the Power Breakfast at the Cracker Barrel

A conversation with four male assistant principals in my office one day left me with a strong message about men working for a female high school principal. One assistant principal had failed to follow proper district procedures concerning a special-education student in a disciplinary matter. Parents were organizing and threatening a 504 complaint. At the suggestion of the district's Director of Special Services and the attorney, I documented the assistant principal's actions and my attempts to correct them in the event of an Office of Civil Rights complaint and investigation. Understandably, the assistant principal was upset, and his colleagues rallied around him.

As we met and shared our frustrations with Public Law 94-142 and the write-up of an employee, one assistant principal verbalized his feelings: "No male wants to screw up for a female boss."

"Is that the issue?" I asked him. I turned to the others and said, "Is he speaking for the rest of you?"

Their responses ranged from silence to a head-shaking, "I-can't-believe-he-said-that-even-if-we-feel-it" look, to one who said, "No one wants to screw up for any boss."

Later, I interviewed a prospective assistant football coach and physical education teacher. When he began listing the references I could contact, I noticed that his immediate supervisor, an athletic director, was a female—almost unheard-of in Southern high schools. Obviously reading my surprise, he volunteered, "Other men often ask me what it's like to work for a female athletic director. I tell them she's the winningest basketball coach I know and the best athletic director I've ever worked for. She's organized and she understands the needs of the football program."

I imagine the men on my staff were often asked what it's like to work for a female principal. I would have preferred it if they had been asked, "What's it like working for Anna?" I suppose the reality is that gender battles still rage in relationships and in the workplace. My observations and experience convince me that these battles are in reality issues of control, indicative of where people are on their individual journeys toward self-actualization. Where individuals find themselves on this journey will determine their response to control issues. Although I'm fully aware that I haven't completed my journey and that I have a long way to go, based on my experience in public education I do have some observations on self-actualized men and women and how they function in relationships in the workplace.

A self-actualized man is one who has taken the time to know himself. He has resolved his issues with his father, and his father or a substitute has now become a wise companion on his journey. The traveler recognizes that his mother, programmed by the culture, might have sent him messages that the purpose of men is to take care of women and that his father was never quite good enough at doing that. He rejects the message and forgives his mother, recognizing the power of the culture to set all this up. He rejects the caretaking of women for two reasons: (1) It places him in the position of allowing a woman to live her life through him—a situation that predestines resentment on his part and prevents a woman from having her own life, and (2) it ultimately is disparaging to women because it keeps them subservient to men. Therefore, in relationships and in the workplace, the self-actualized man is neither threatened nor intimidated by a successful woman. Instead, he values her worth and being, expecting her not to take care of all his needs but to walk beside him on their individual journeys.

Like the self-actualized man, the self-actualized woman has resolved her family-of-origin issues. She has discovered those parts of herself that are like her mother, has analyzed the script written for her, and has begun writing the script for her own life. She rejects the cultural definition of female happiness—finding the right man—for an authentic definition: "When you don't need a man, you're ready for a relationship." She chooses a career based on her intuition and calmly but deliberately works to eliminate any barriers in her way.

In the workplace, and particularly in the female high school principalship, such a woman rejects the codependent expectations of female as caretaker. She responds to demands and manipulation with a gentle self-reminder, "This is not about me." Yet she has compassion for those who struggle with their journey toward self-actualization. Her goal in leading others is fostering their own self-responsibility. Women's healthy assuming of responsibility for their own actions can, I hope, influence the same in all the students in their care.

Self-actualization is the goal. As a female high school principal, I realized I had not arrived. On good days, I had glimpses of such possibilities. On bad days, I realized that my own gender participates in activities that perpetuate covert female power structures while hindering the self-actualization process.

In my community, a group of female parents who worked in the home gathered every Thursday morning for their ritual Power Breakfast at the Cracker Barrel—the Southern female answer to lunch at the Top of the Mart. Stories of this event fascinated me and affected me both personally and professionally.

It is interesting to ponder how men and women in the South have agreed to be. Southern women know about power. In the suburban South, they have adapted to covert power at the bridge table, the tennis court, and in my community, the Power Breakfast.

The Power Breakfast began with a core group of financially secure females with children in my school. I greatly respected this core group. They had their own lives, volunteered at school, but didn't attempt to live their lives through their kids. One became our district Volunteer of the Year.

However, during my last year as principal, the group expanded to include a few individuals with a different agenda. One in particular, an old friend of mine, began using the group for various purposes: to discuss who should run for student body president (she was dismayed when an African American female won); who were the good and bad teachers; what was wrong with Anna Hicks as a principal; and who knew what about the personal lives of teachers, principals, and even school board members. A few of the core members became disenchanted and had the courage to inform me and other targets about what was happening. At the age of 42, I learned some painful lessons about the betrayal of false friends.

Like a few other females, I had dared to be different. We could not accept covert power. Most Southern males accepted us as long as we didn't "show them up." Anyone who dares to break such a tacit agreement with either sex puts herself at risk. This experience taught me a great deal.

I discovered that we live in a time when "sexism" and "sexual discrimination" are terms that are bantered about with a looseness that is potentially dangerous to real progress in resolving gender issues. My experience as a female high school principal in a male-dominated hierarchy taught me that there is a major difference between cultural gender stereotypes and sexism.

Cultural gender stereotypes are not the exclusive purview of males and are not necessarily pathological. I previously described the superintendent who discouraged my pursuit of the principalship. He clearly operated from these stereotypes, but once I was hired, he was fully supportive. He never attributed problems in my school to my gender. Paradoxically perhaps, my greatest conflicts with cultural gender stereotypes arose from other women (the Cracker Barrel crowd). The dialogue at these meets was often an attempt to balance the power of females occupying nontraditional roles. The back-stabbing behavior was the pathological side of cultural gender stereotypes and represented a covert threat to the female principal that was probably more powerful

than the ill-disguised, overtly sexist acts of the superintendent who hired me.

The other superintendent I worked for was outwardly as
nonsexist as one could be, yet I and other females were
targets of his temper tantrums that resulted in verbally abusive one-way conversations. I cannot say for certain that
males did not receive similar treatment. If they did, they
were too embarrassed to speak up when the principals got
together. This type of sexism is not identified by any sexist
language or remarks but is pathological, being born of a
male-dominance/female-subservience motif of long standing. I am admittedly threatened by loud, abusive talk and it
disarms me. It is only afterward that I engage in the "I wish
I'd saids" and the other "shoulds" and "oughts" that women
sometimes use on themselves to prolong their suffering.

The movement toward equality in the workplace must
be a bipartisan effort. Men must move away from insisting
that women adopt their "kick butt" and "I'll demonstrate it
by kicking yours" style of leadership. Women must learn to
detach from this type of behavior and not take it personally.
Men who successfully operate in capitalistic hierarchies
have learned to depersonalize such behavior as simply part
of the game. Women must learn to do the same to survive but
must also realize the value of their ability in leadership roles
to lead in a more humane manner. For the female principalship, support for the person trying to be both humane and
courageous is essential.

14

From Whence Cometh My Help?

Principals are lonely people. It is indeed lonely at the top. It took me a year to accept this reality and to finally begin to build a support system. It was the only reason I survived.

The first support I sought was from individuals. Within the system, I experienced tremendous support from the director of special services, a Ph.D. in psychology who later became personnel director and left the district when I did. He frequently played the unofficial therapist role for district employees. When I was going through my divorce years earlier, he eased my guilt with these powerful words: "Anna, sometimes divorce can be therapeutic." In my role as principal, he affirmed and supported me in some tough personnel issues, constantly reminding me that sometimes we need to get rid of employees to protect children or when it is in the best interests of the district.

Outside the system, another great source of support was my Episcopal priest. I first met him when he served on a district committee I chaired on a controversial thinking-skills program. Searching for a new church home, I joined his parish, where he became my priest and my friend. I discovered that being a priest is very like being a principal—that is, being everything to everybody, sometimes pleasing no one, and struggling to take care of yourself. He introduced me to the power of reflection and daily meditation, though I freely admit I often lacked the self-discipline to reap the benefits.

At the end of my first year as principal, I discovered the power of group support. Nominated by one of my university mentors, I attended the first National Principals' Academy sponsored by the University of Delaware and the Education Commission of the States. We were chosen on the basis of reputation as risk-taking principals, and there I met some of the most fascinating people I have ever known: a female principal of an Eskimo village school in Alaska who exposed a village council cover-up of child abuse; a long, tall, chain-smoking Texan principal of an Hispanic school with some of the highest test scores in the state; a female high school principal of a suburban New Mexico high school whose school was 2 years ahead of me in the fight to reform the American high school; a roller-blading, renegade Louisiana elementary principal making a name for himself with school innovation; an intense, compulsive, extremely creative female principal of a K-12 school leading the way in Kentucky's famous education reform; a slow-talking male Southern high school principal from Alabama, determined to change the academy agenda and lead the charge; and a male Hispanic high school principal of one of the first Coalition schools in the nation. These were just a few of the 43-member class who descended on Newark, Delaware. It was a life-changing experience for me professionally.

The change began with our experience-on-the-ropes course designed to make us a team and encourage risk-taking. I actually got up the nerve and climbed 25 feet to the top of a pamper pole, stood and rotated on a pizza-sized disk, and then sailed to the ground harnessed to ropes and straps held securely by my group. Such an experience convinced me of the joy of living for possibilities.

The other powerful experience during those 3 weeks in Delaware was the presence of Ted Sizer. I had already asked the faculty and staff at my school to read *Horace's School* (Sizer, 1992). The book was incredible, but the chance to work in a small group with the author brought the book to life. Sizer modeled what he professed in the book—the educator as scholar—not just lecturing to the principals in the room but raising questions, hearing our responses, and supporting our reflection and the uniqueness of each of our schools. My product in the class was a development of a design for change for my school to begin the conversation concerning the Coalition of Essential Schools and the Nine Common Principles. It was the guideline for my reform attempts for the next 3 years.

Our National Principals Academy Class has followed up each year with a reunion and renewal at the annual Association of Supervision and Curriculum Development convention. It is interesting that a few of us either have left the principalship, gone on sabbatical, been promoted to central office, or retired. I now have a lifetime network of friends around the nation who have been there, who understood the loneliness, and who all care about kids.

Fortunately, I found a similar group close to home in our own District Principals' Association. We actually began meeting monthly for lunch, elected a president, and called in agenda items for each meeting. The value of this venture was that the 15 of us never engaged in budget competition or backbiting. As the school board became sometimes divisive and as our district leadership began to turn over rapidly, we suddenly became afraid to be seen having lunch together. *Administrator* seemed more and more to be a dirty word, especially in the eyes of the local Senior Citizens for Tax Relief group. We discovered we still needed each other and began meeting in our homes in the evenings. I remember vividly an evening when one principal called us together in great distress, and we listened to her experience and heartache. A male principal wrote me later to thank me for hosting the group and to tell me that he was uncomfortable sharing his pain but felt comforted to know he was not alone. I became convinced then of the power of a group of coworkers in supporting each other.

I've often said that the principalship was the hardest job I've ever loved. On reflection, I now realize that one of the reasons I loved the job so was the caring, compassionate people who cared for me; I'll never forget them. But there were many times when I was forced to take care of myself.

My principalship training prepared me well for many aspects of the job. The classroom and practicum experiences, as well as the advice of my mentors, were invaluable. But no one prepared me for one of the most vital parts of the job—taking care of myself. And I've come to realize that no one else could.

A woman's guilt is powerful in the high school principalship. She brings to the role the collective guilt of her sex: that of not being able to be everything to everybody. The strong tendency of women to mother or parent those in their charge can place a female principal in the precarious position of trying to take care of everyone else at the expense of taking care of herself. The result is that nothing is left either for those she loves or, more important, for herself. I call this dilemma the "Stress Trap." I've been caught in the trap on more than one occasion and know the symptoms well.

The physical symptoms are lethargy and irritability, and occasionally feeling like a top that's been wound so tightly that it cannot even begin to spin in release. My strongest emotional clue is getting my feelings hurt easily and falling into a victimization pattern. This telltale sign is my signal to look around and organize myself to stop my world long enough to care about me.

Caring about myself during the principalship sometimes meant time away from school and home. I used to try simply to take time away from school, but the phone still rang, and my children's demands continued, and the stress never left. I finally learned to go away, most often to the South Carolina coast, where I found my solace in reading and writing.

When I first went away, I called school, hoping to ease my guilt and worrying as to what would occur in my absence. I finally learned not to call but simply to trust those in charge to handle whatever occurred. In my absence, they handled a fire between the floors, a major fight, and a special-education student who fled the campus down a major highway. One realization I now have is that principals have to give up control to enable those they supervise to grow and lead. I used to apologize for going away if an incident occurred. Somehow, time and permission to take care of myself eventually convinced me no apologies were necessary.

Those days on the South Carolina coast were the most healing time of my principalship. The more remote areas of this Southern treasure are havens for weary souls seeking wholeness and some connection with a higher power. In utter defiance of my mother's warnings against skin cancer, I immersed myself in the warmth of the lazy summer sun. For a few hours, time stood still, and I found myself ready for reentry into the system of school administration.

I've now decided that the purpose of work is our creative, expressive opportunity to participate and contribute to a larger sense of community. Retirement, then (years away for me), is our reward—the expansion of the time in our working life when we pause to care for ourselves. Retirement is a time not to fear or postpone, but to treasure and anticipate as a thank-you from the culture. My fantasy at the age of 42 centers around a contented retirement, knowing that I worked in a profession where I had a chance to make a difference every single day. With that knowledge, as a principal, I began to long for that time and for anonymity—to attend church as any other parishioner and not as the high school principal having to hear the parental complaint from the pew in front; to be able to linger in the Fresh Market over the gourmet coffee and be completely ignored by other shoppers; to lounge in the sun at the swim club, uninterrupted by parents wanting to introduce themselves to complain about a teacher.

Slowly, I have discovered as a principal that my strong private self is powerfully emerging to take the place of a now-weary public self. But it will take time for my private self and me to get reacquainted—or perhaps I should say to develop a new relationship based on a new appreciation. Before becoming a principal, I took my privacy for granted. Now it is precious and deserving of protection. It is, I suppose, like every other treasure. Once it has been threatened, we guard it with a tenacity that previously seemed unnecessary. I often found myself on guard with the press, but a principal must at times be a public self and find the balance.

15

Who's Afraid
of the Press?

On my coffee table sits a history of the community in which I served as principal. A gift from its author, a former editor of the local newspaper, it is inscribed, "To Anna Hicks, I've always been a fan of the underdog."

After I had been on the job a few weeks, my selection as principal was the subject of headlines in the local paper. A letter to the editor suggested that my selection was based on favoritism by the committee. An article in the paper raised similar concerns. Having been a newspaper sponsor, I believed deeply in the freedom of the press, and I also felt strongly about a responsible press. In this situation, I could not sit back. I called the editor to meet me for lunch.

The editor was someone most people in the school district avoided. He had a witty, cynical style that could pierce even the thickest skin. I was perhaps more innocent then, but I believed in my ability to appeal to this man's intelligence and reason. When we met, I was pleasant but up-front. "If you're going to write about me," I said, "I want you to at least know who I am."

He then showed me an anonymous letter he had not printed that also objected to my selection. After reading it, I recognized the style—that of a teacher I had begun documenting for dismissal when I served as assistant principal for instruction. I proceeded to tell the editor my story of my quest for the principalship. I must have convinced him that I was an underdog candidate. He never printed the anonymous letter, but he sent me his book and later read and reviewed in the paper, at my request, Sizer's *Horace's School* (1992) when our school began our Coalition of Essential Schools conversations.

The statewide paper was a greater challenge. The first reporter with whom I worked was a great disappointment. I finally determined that her unwillingness to verify information was a simple matter of laziness. She was the only member of the press who ever truly angered me. The incident that set me off concerned a major faux pas on the part of the district's food service manager, who placed in the cafeteria (without my knowledge) a fruit drink that looked exactly like a wine cooler and a display sign that read, "For the Designated Driver." I had not seen the drink or the display until an angry parent called to complain. Her point was well-taken and I began steps to remove the beverage. The parent, however, couldn't wait until the next day to see if the problem had been resolved and called the paper. The story ran the next day without any attempt by the writer to get information from the school. I was livid.

The executive editor of the paper had been running on weekends a column explaining changes in the paper and soliciting feedback from the readership. So I called, made an appointment, and presented myself in his office to share my concerns. I indicated my willingness to always cooperate with the press but told him that if a story concerned my school, I hoped that someone would contact me or my designee. A true professional, he defended his reporter but listened sensitively to my comments. The reporter left the paper a few months later.

The reporter I most respected covered my school for the last 2 years of my principalship. I regarded her highly as a journalist—she was bright, insightful, and never missed an opportunity for a good story. For some reason, we liked and admired each other. I always returned her calls and felt free to initiate contact. Even with sensitive personnel issues, although she would dig for information, she understood my legal and ethical need to be silent. When I left the principalship, I nominated her for the Benjamin Fine Award for Outstanding Education Reporting given by the National Association of Secondary School Principals. She was the best example of the press as a principal's best critical friend.

16

The High School
Principal as Parent

Being a principal has taught me much about parenting. Parenting also has influenced my work as a principal. The principalship is the hardest job I've ever loved for
which I was trained. Parenting is the toughest challenge I've
ever faced with no training to prepare me.

I am the divorced mother of three daughters: a 16-year-
old rising junior named Mary Anna and identical twin girls,
Sallie and Elizabeth, who are entering the seventh grade. My
career in public education and the time I have devoted to my
graduate work have robbed the girls of time with their
mother. I'd like to think that although they know this, they
celebrate our moments together. The four of us share the
same large expressive eyes as, and hopeless love for, our
female Cocker Spaniel, who rules the home and our hearts.
The man in my life calls her my inner child, the little unin-
hibited girl I was never allowed to be.

The dog had no clue that I was a high school principal.
The children, however, were powerfully aware, and their
reactions varied. The oldest, Mary Anna, a natural beauty by
her mother's and the public's standards, was painfully
aware of her mother's vocation. She was fiercely independent like her mother, and it became clear in her middle
school years that the prospect of being a student in a school
where her mother was principal threatened her happiness

and identity. For this reason, the summer prior to her fresh-
man year, I built a home in the attendance area of the new
high school in our district so that my daughter could be her
own person. I am amazed at the number of times I was called
upon to explain placing my child in another school. Our
family's personal decisions often seemed to become matters
of public interest. As my oldest child said, "Everyone seems
to make our business their business." Even with the change
of schools, I found there were times when my daughter's
confidentiality was violated by her own teachers.

The twins are an adventurous, extroverted, energetic
pair who were loyal devotees of their mother's school and
athletic teams. They find fun and often mischief wherever
they go. At the age of 12, they would have been most content
to attend Mom's school, but my strong desire for their independent school experience compelled me to forgo the privilege I enjoyed as a district employee to place them in my
school's attendance area and, instead, to send them in the
direction of their sister. They, too, deserved the chance to live
their own lives outside the shadow of their mother.

A friend once told me that most of life is "just showing
up." What you are to do once you get there is usually determined by others. The same friend also contends that 90% of
parenting is simply being there for our kids and the other
10% is listening to them so we will know when they need us
to be there. I have seen many kids in my office whose problems were parents who either were not there for them or
were too present, overpowering, or suffocating in their lives.
My greatest frustration in the parent-principal role was trying to be there for my kids when the job told me to be
somewhere else for someone else's kids, the ones I was hired
to serve. I struggled frequently in attempting to maintain a
proper balance in this professional tug-of-war.

I felt at times responsible for so many children. My heart
often ached with a message so many needed to hear. In the
words of Joseph Campbell, "Follow your bliss" (Osborn,
1991, p. 16). Life is an adventure to be lived to its fullest.
Listen to the voice within you. Be guided not by the masses
nor by the tide of the culture, but by your own intuition.

Reject roles in the sometimes well-meaning scripts written for your lives. Confront your own resentment. Resentment is a killer. Build a life you can live without it. I hope my own children and some of the children in my professional care will enjoy such a future.

17

Upon Reflection

My long-term goal is to live one day in an arrogantly shabby beach house on the South Carolina coast and continue writing. What I hope to savor in those days to come are special moments so powerful that they kept me going during the trying times in the principalship. Some were light, some were sorrowful, but all were memorable.

During my first year as principal, I joined the students at lunch one day in the cafeteria and sat next to a little ninth-grade boy. He looked at me and asked, "Who are you?"

"I'm Anna Hicks, the principal," I replied.

"You mean the head principal?" he asked in disbelief.

"Yes," I said. "I'm in charge of the whole place."

"You can't be," he insisted.

Realizing I couldn't convince him, I pulled out my proof, my official high school athletic association pass with my name and title and permission to enter all athletic contests for free. He then grinned sheepishly, shook my hand, and said, "Pleased to meet you."

About that same time, while patrolling the halls one day, I encountered four large males—obviously nonstudents—sneaking into a side entrance of the school. "May I help you?" I inquired.

"We have an appointment with the principal," they boasted.

"Oh, really?" I said. "I'm the principal and I'm through with my appointments for the day." They took off running.

Another day while wandering the halls, I felt the need to escape. That day had been full of petty problems perceived as crises by the people owning the problems. I crossed the bus traffic circle at the technology center next door where several special education programs were also housed. I found my way to the Profoundly Mentally Handicapped Class where the teacher and her assistant were feeding, diapering, and working to visually stimulate the children. I watched intently as the teacher fed one child and spoke with pride about the progress the child had made in feeding—accepting the spoon and swallowing. He was 9 years old. I left the classroom, found a deserted stairwell, and wept for the students and parents in my middle-class school who didn't have a clue and for my own misdirected self-pity.

Humor always helped on darker days. I loved to act and make a fool of myself. The students especially seemed to enjoy it. One colder-than-usual Friday, I actually donned a diver's wet suit and became a willing target in a dunking booth fundraiser for the student council. I hit the water at least six times and raised a respectable sum of money, breaking a solid Southern rule: Never show your head wet except at the swim club.

My favorite role, however, was the finale of Faculty Follies—a fundraiser for needy students. I organized and recruited faculty and staff (it's hard to say "no" to the principal) for a skit dedicated to the senior class entitled, "The Twelve Years of School." To the tune of "The Twelve Days of Christmas," it went something like this:

In my first year of school, my mother said to me,
Don't wet your panties and don't embarrass me.

I played the first grader who came out singing the aforementioned lyrics and was then joined by teachers and staff members appropriately dressed and singing the following:

In my second year of school, Don't throw a tantrum.
Third year of school, Don't get dirty.
Fourth year of school, Don't spitball the teacher.
Fifth year of school, Don't chase the boys.

Sixth year of school, Don't chew gum.
Seventh year of school, Don't wear too much makeup.
Eighth year of school, Don't wear short skirts.
Ninth year of school, Don't flirt with seniors.
Tenth year of school, Don't wreck the car.
Eleventh year of school, Don't get arrested.
Twelfth year of school, Don't embarrass me at graduation.

We were a hit, and our performance was preserved on video. It still airs for student enjoyment and great embarrassment to many.

Many faculty members exhibited this sense of team spirit. I was fortunate to hire many good people. One of my best memories was hiring a former student. Having grown up professionally for 18 years in the school where I became principal, I had been privileged to teach many fine students in my English and journalism classes. Last year, I hired a former English student who brought to the classroom energy, enthusiasm, respect for kids, and the willingness to be a risk taker. I realized at that point what others had described to me as the professional cycle—the student becomes the teacher. And at some point we begin to see ourselves as mentors in the profession.

My mentoring experiences were many, but my most rewarding was serving as a site supervisor to female South African High School Principals' Practicum students involved in an exchange program with the Department of Educational Leadership and Policy at the University of South Carolina. I supervised two courageous women who were a part of a second revolution in South Africa—the fight for the equality of women. I attended a luncheon for the practicum supervisors of these students and listened in wonder as they sang in beautiful harmony their native songs and their national anthem. They spoke with sadness of their homesickness but with gratitude for their experience in America.

Near the end of my last year as principal, the newspaper sponsor stopped by the office to ask if I would attend with her and the staff a Scholastic Press Association luncheon where one of her students would be named Journalist of the

Year in the state. I gladly accepted, remembering fondly my days as a newspaper sponsor. As we watched the awards ceremony, I suddenly heard an award being given to a former newspaper sponsor who became a principal but who always respected the freedom of the press. I then heard my name called to accept the Scroggins Award given by the College of Journalism at the University of South Carolina and the South Carolina Scholastic Press Association for outstanding contributions to high school journalism. I realized then the legacy I left—a firm belief in the value and worth of the freedom of the student press.

What I treasure most, upon reflection, is the letter I received from a student when I decided to leave the principalship:

Dear Dr. Hicks,

Before moving to South Carolina, I attended a high school about the same size as this one. To be honest, I don't even remember the principal's name. I doubt he ever ate lunch with the student body. He never stood at the main entrance to greet us in the morning. He was a disciplinarian, a dictator, not someone students felt comfortable waving or talking to.

I can, however, honestly say that our school will be at a loss next year without you. It is obvious that you care about this school. Not many people agreed with the scheduling changes you proposed. I know I didn't. But I know you were doing what you thought was best. You worked with the Key Club to get their initiation back, and you fought to get the warning bell back as well.

I'm going to miss high school next year (with the exception of Pre-Calculus). I am glad I got to attend our school while you were still principal. Being on the newspaper staff this year gave me an even greater respect for you. You take a lot of criticism from us, and unlike some principals, you have yet to exercise your right to censor us.

I wanted you to know that you haven't gone unappreciated. I think you are an asset to our school and wish you the best of luck next year. I look forward to reading your book.

Bridget

18

A Lady Always Knows
When to Leave

My mother taught me to be a lady. And in the South, being a lady is essential. Some lessons I learned and some I didn't. For instance, when I left for college, my mother advised me to learn to play bridge, tennis, and the organ. (It's always nice to be able to fill in at church services.) I never took an interest in any of these activities. Some lessons, however, I learned so well that I find myself repeating them to my three daughters: Never leave the house without your makeup and your hair in place. Never wear white shoes before Easter or after Labor Day. When life is tough, hold your head up and walk tall. And most important of all, never wear out your welcome—a lady always knows when to leave.

My decision to leave the principalship at the end of my fourth year was an intuitive one, a decision based on knowing when to leave. There were signs along the way in that last year that, as I look back, convince me that decision was a wise one.

I have determined that any time we are trying to decide if it's time to leave, a detailed analysis of what is happening at work really isn't necessary. The only thing we really need to analyze is what happens to our bodies the first 15 seconds after the alarm clock goes off.

Educators have been brainwashed. We believe that because the mind is the keeper of knowledge, it is also the center of consciousness. Not so! The center of consciousness is the body, which informs the mind. Our body knows when something does not "feel right" long before our intellect processes the whys and wherefores.

This does not mean we should merely act on or react to our feelings in important matters. It does mean, however, that we should not act against them. We should not let our minds try to talk our bodies out of their feelings. As a friend once said, such action is an express train to Prozac.

I began to ask myself, "What is there specifically about this job that produces this general ill feeling when the alarm clock goes off?" Identifying this connection resulted in an epiphany for me. From a therapeutic perspective, it created what noted therapist Carl Whitaker (1989) calls "an existential shift" (pp. 52-54).

Whitaker's idea is well illustrated in the story of the woman who decides to leave her husband because she cannot be married to a man who parks in handicapped spaces. The epiphany here is the sureness in this very powerful metaphor that the relative value systems of the two people are in irreconcilable conflict. The existential shift is the realization that, having this awareness, a continuation of this relationship would assign to one's life an inauthenticity of pathological proportions.

For me, the epiphany was my realization that my leadership style is an extension of who I am. I found myself, after considerable turnover in the district office staff, being expected to adopt a leadership style that was more directive and controlling than my own natural style. I realized that to adopt another person's style would make me an extension of that individual and his or her philosophy, and essentially would make me a nonperson. This reality was unacceptable and so far out of touch with my understanding of what constitutes a professional that I had no choice but to change to a healthier environment.

Leaving can be scary. We want the epiphany without the existential shift. We can't have one without the other.

My decision was aided by an offer. In San Francisco at an Association for Supervision and Curriculum Development meeting at which I was presenting, I attended a reunion of the first class of the National Principals' Academy sponsored by the University of Delaware. Having attended the first class, I had been invited back the following summer as a presenter on leadership and school reform. A faculty member and consultant approached me in San Francisco with an offer to join him in consulting work to provide leadership and team-building training to principals, schools, and district office staffs. I said I would consider it.

I returned from my trip and contacted the University of South Carolina Department of Educational Leadership and Policy to be certain I could continue my clinical faculty position. The answer was yes, and I was asked to teach their personnel and leadership courses. Consulting, therefore, seemed a viable option.

When contracts were issued in the district, I returned mine unsigned with a letter of resignation after 21 years of service as a teacher and administrator in the school district. I made the official announcement to the faculty. A few teachers were no doubt elated (those whom I had had to reprimand). Others cried, some sent flowers, two took me to dinner and gave me a Tom Clarke "School Marm" gnome, the principals in the district threw me a party, and the district office employees with whom I worked when I was language arts coordinator took me out.

My parting gift from the faculty was a three-quarter carat diamond necklace in the shape of a heart. The card said, "Our heart goes with you." The department heads, knowing my love for flowers, gave me a crystal vase. The superintendent recognized me at a board meeting with a plaque for 21 years of service in the district.

A new principal, a friend of mine and the first African American principal in the district, was hired. A parent called to tell me that people were asking if the school was ready for a Black principal. I responded abruptly that such a question was certainly inappropriate in 1995. I remembered, also, a similar question being asked about me as a female when I was hired 4 years earlier. I hope that in some small way I broke through some barriers and that his path will be easier.

It's a hot July in South Carolina as I bathe in the sun at the swim club pool. I'm glad to no longer be principal, but I treasure the time I spent in the hardest job I ever loved. I recall with mixed emotions my last day on the job. A friend gave me a hot pink T-shirt to wear that said, "I Can Do Anything I Want On My Last Day." And so I did.

I finished packing, reminded the head custodian to clean my office and shampoo the carpet for the new principal, and wrote my last memo to the district office—a tactful reminder that the building must be painted in preparation for the Blue Ribbon Schools site visit in the fall. The administrative staff and I then enjoyed lunch at a local restaurant and returned to load my car.

I turned in my keys, including the key to the gym, to the head custodian. On reflection, I realized I had used that key to open the gym on only two occasions. I learned in my 4 years as principal something very powerful: Keys are symbols of control and symbols of responsibility. If I had not had a key to the gym, I would no doubt have needed it on a regular basis. This is the paradox of control: Those who do not have it try desperately to obtain it, and those who have it seldom have to exercise it.

We live in a world of epidemic insecurity. The more insecure we feel, the more locks we install. The more locks we install, the more keys we carry and the more time and energy we spend letting ourselves in and out of our self-made prisons. In short, the more we seek security from the forces outside us, the more those forces control us, until we reach the point of trading our personal power for external control over something that has less and less value to us.

The gifts and expressions I received at my parting served to remind me of something very important. Although many doors were slammed in my face, I was able to open others through which those who follow may, I hope, walk unimpeded. The keys to those doors I brought with me to the job, and I take them with me as I leave. They cannot be duplicated or allocated to others. They were forged from my own courage, tempered by the wisdom of my mentors, and they remain aglow in the fires of my spirit. There they await reshaping through the sound of my still-soft voice in search of new doors to open.

References

Brown, J. F. (1909). *The American high school*. Norwood, MA: J. S. Cushing/Berwick and Smith.

Malone, T. P., & Malone, P. T. (1987). *The art of intimacy*. New York: Prentice-Hall.

Osbon, D. K. (Ed.). (1991). *Reflections on the art of living: A Joseph Campbell companion*. New York: HarperCollins.

Sizer, T. R. (1992). *Horace's school: Redesigning the American high school*. Boston: Houghton Mifflin.

Whitaker, C. A. (1989). *Midnight musings of a family therapist*. New York: Norton.

**CORWIN
PRESS**

The Corwin Press logo—a raven striding across an open book—represents the happy union of courage and learning. We are a professional-level publisher of books and journals for K–12 educators, and we are committed to creating and providing resources that embody these qualities. Corwin's motto is "Success for All Learners."